W9-BFK-967

A Small Group Curriculum for Girls

THRIVE

IN THE HIVE

Surviving The Girl's World of Good and Bad Relationship Bee-haviors

By Stephanie Jensen, MS

youth light inc.

© 2013 by YouthLight, Inc. | Chapin, SC 29036

Layout and Design by Melody Taylor/GraphicSolutions, Inc.
Project Editing by Susan Bowman

Library of Congress Control Number: 2013954248
ISBN: 9781598501483

10 9 8 7 6 5 4 3 2 1
Printed in the United States

Dedication

This book is dedicated to my two beautiful daughters, Emma and Landis, who provide ongoing inspiration to address the problem of relational aggression. Thank you both for sharing your experiences, struggles and successes in friendships. The friendship you have with each other is beautiful and should be cherished. You girls are becoming lovely young women and I am proud of each of you.

Acknowledgments

This book would not have been possible without the support of the following individuals:

Susan Bowman, thank you for believing in me and pushing me for two years to put my thoughts and ideas to paper.

Dr. Ellen Shrouf, your guidance and patience listening to my ideas and my struggles pushed me to stay focused and make this dream a reality.

Boys Town, without the amazing services, care and support this agency offers children, families and the staff that serves them I would not have been able to apply my knowledge and experiences held in these pages.

Finally, my wonderful family, I would be nothing without your love and laughter. My amazing husband, thank you for letting me bounce "girly" ideas off of you and offering your creative advice! Austin, Emma and Laney, my three wonderful and amazing children, thanks for giving me time to focus my thoughts on this project and for offering stories and ideas.

TABLE OF CONTENTS

INTRODUCTION

It's a beautiful spring afternoon and you are sitting on a park bench enjoying the sights, sounds and smells of a warm day. The flowers are in bloom, the birds are chirping and everything is right with the world. And then you hear a familiar sound near your head that strikes fear in your heart. A buzz that gets louder and you turn to see a bee buzzing around you. Whoa, the scene changes! Your peaceful afternoon has quickly transformed into a horrific event. Think of your last encounter with a honey bee. Ask anyone about the last time a bee was buzzing around their head and the response will not require words for you to understand how they felt about being in close proximity to a bee!

Switch settings, it's the first day of seventh grade. You set foot into your first class and all your friends are there. You are chatting excitedly and catching up on all the important news since summer break when SHE walks in. She gives a look that promptly puts a stop to all conversation that does not revolve around her and she takes her place in the seat right next to you. Have you had an encounter with a pre-teen or teenage girl like this...did you have a similar reaction as you did to the bee? Most people fear bees because of their sting and would prefer to stay far away from them-even though they have never been stung. The same holds true with many young girls. Did you know that 70% of girls report having been mistreated by their friends and for girls aged 8 to 17, when asked what actually worried them the most, the number one concern, was being teased or being made fun of. (The Girl Scout Research Institute, Feeling Safe: What Girls Say (2003). Wow! That sounds like a lot of stinging in the girls' world! Did you also know that this stinging business (whether by words or stinger) is reserved for females? Yes, male bees cannot sting, and in the human world, girls engage in the stinging effects of "relational aggression" at much higher rates than their male counterparts.

Did you know that 70% of girls report having been mistreated by their friends?

Being a teenage girl in today's world can be tough! While girls and boys deal with many of the same issues; there are certain issues unique to the experience of growing up as a girl in this society. Helping girls navigate the tumultuous adolescent years and feel a sense of belonging in their families, with their peers, and in their communities, enables them to be emotionally balanced, self-assured, and better able to deal with challenges and difficulties. During adolescence, girls' social life is greatly focused on, their friendships and the value of being accepted within a social group. They begin to develop powerful friendship bonds which create close, personal bonds with one another. While powerful, these friendship bonds are fluid and fragile, and are rarely stable over time (Harris, 1995; Savin-Williams, 1980; Simmons, 2002). A study of the friendship bonds among a group of girls aged 10 to 12 years old, (Besag, 2006: 535), found that girls considered their friendships extremely important and identified the breaking of a friendship as the most anxiety-provoking aspect of school life.

While there is no question that girls have a strong desire to belong to a group, this belonging can be very painful without appropriate support and friendships. One negative aspect of being part of a group of friends is pressure to look or act in a certain way in order to continue to be part of the group. Girls may be willing to do things that go against their beliefs or that they really don't want to do in order to maintain their place in the group. Belonging to a group can help girls feel more secure however, the best security is found from within rather than from others.

How to Use This Book

Adapted from the work of Rosalind Wiseman in her book, *Queen Bees and Wannabes*, these activities explore the seven (7) different roles that girls assume within the structure of a social clique. These roles make up the social fabric within the clique – or hive as we will refer to it – and determine how each child will influence or impact relationships with the others around them. Adolescent social structures can be very complex and sophisticated. Within the group, roles and positions are not static, they can change frequently. This book explores the similarities in bee-haviors and the social hierarchy of the honey bee with adolescent girls in an effort to better understand how girls relate to each other and how they can "thrive in the hive." Activities can be used as standalone or as an eight week girls' group. If time allows, there are additional activities included in the Appendix at the end of this book.

Providing safe spaces for girls to discuss the climate of their friendships is important; more important is encouraging them to develop ways to move beyond discussion and give them room and power to initiate change. In our hive, there are no two bees that are exactly alike and each of us should strive to improve ourselves, the bees/peers that live and study alongside of us and as a wholework to make our hive one that is thriving and free of relational aggression and bullying..

Tips for Leaders

So, you're ready to start a group, now you need participants! One important key to a successful group is doing your homework on your participants before signing them up-this is especially true when working with pre-teen and teenage girls. Whether the girls are teacher referred, parent referred or self-referred it is important for you to meet with each potential candidate before developing your group. Spend 10-15 minutes with each girl prior to forming the group to evaluate how she might interact with the rest of the girls being considered. You will want a balance of outspoken and quiet girls, girls from different friend groups and girls with diverse backgrounds. An even mixture of personalities and temperaments will deepen the discussions and allow each girl to stretch and grow. Once you have identified a group of girls that you think will work well together send them a formal invitation to participate in the group with the meeting date and time. Make the invitation special so they know they are part of something special! Ask them to RSVP by a specific date. Once you have your group confirmed, send a letter to parents/guardians explaining the group goals and obtain permission for their daughter to participate. A sample permission form can be found at the end of the book.

SESSION 1
Hive Jive

Getting Started:

Girls love to talk. A recent study from the University of Maryland School of Medicine (Paddock, 2013) found that girls' brains produce more of a language protein than boys. On average girls will utter 20,000 words a day compared to 7,000 words spoken by boys. When working with girls in a group setting it is important to set clear boundaries and expectations about healthy communication and confidentiality to guide their discussions for a rewarding group experience for all members. The following activities introduce the girls to the expectations of group communication and to each other in a positive, interactive way.

On average girls will utter 20,000 words a day compared to 7,000 words spoken by boys.

ACTIVITY 1.1
The Buzz

PURPOSE: Group members will learn about each other and communicate something about themselves to begin getting comfortable sharing and discussing personal topics.

OBJECTIVES: Group members will:

1. Learn positive attributes about each other.

2. Learn the T.H.I.N.K. Model when communicating with each other.

RESOURCES/MATERIALS:

Index cards • Pens/pencils all the same color

PROCEDURES:

1. Distribute index cards.

2. Instruct girls to write a headline about themselves. For example, if you were the subject of a newspaper article or the chapter of a book, what would the headline read?

3. Under their headline ask them to write three statements about themselves. One must be a true statement. The other two must be untrue. (The more outrageous all three statements are the better. Encourage students to think of odd information about themselves that no one would be able to know if it were true or false.)

4. Have the girls put all their cards in a hat or bowl and have one group member draw a card and read it aloud. After all three statements have been read, have the girls vote on which statement they believe to be true. Then have the girl in question reveal the truthful statement and explain their headline.

Close this activity by praising the girls for their willingness to share and learn about each other. Tell them that throughout the group they will be asked to share about themselves and will learn about each other. Let them know that within the group there are expectations they will be asked to follow when communicating.

✳ **A good model is T.H.I.N.K. (from Girl Talk) before you speak: T: True** (is what you are saying true) in the activity we shared some information that was not true about ourselves, this was fun as an activity, but when people say things about us that are untrue it can be hurtful. In this group we want to protect each other and only share things that we know to be true. **H: Helpful** (Are your words helpful or hurtful to the conversation?). **I: Important** (Is what you are about to say important to the topic or is it something that could be discussed later?). **N: Necessary** (Is the information you want to share necessary to continue the conversation?). **K: Kind** (Are your words kind?) Keeping these rules of communication visible for girls can be helpful and you can refer to them to keep the discussion on topic.

THE
T.H.I.N.K.
MODEL

True
Helpful
Important
Necessary
Kind

ACTIVITY 1.2
The Toothpaste Test

PURPOSE: Introduce the importance of maintaining confidentiality in the group and in friendships.

OBJECTIVES: Group members will:

1. Learn how difficult it is to take words back once they have been spoken.

2. Understand the importance of confidentiality in building healthy friendships.

RESOURCES/MATERIALS:

Tube of toothpaste • Paper plate • Wooden stir sticks

PROCEDURES:

1. Take the tube of toothpaste and explain to the group that the toothpaste represents the words and stories that are shared in group or in a friendship.

2. Ask the girls if they have ever been in a situation when someone shared something about them that they asked to keep secret, or if they have ever told something about someone that they had been asked to keep private. Explain to them that confidentiality means maintaining someone's confidence or friendship by keeping private conversations private. During group discussions we might share information about ourselves that we want to stay only within the group. This means we are expecting the girls to keep information shared in the group confidential.

3. Open the tube of toothpaste and begin to squeeze it out on the paper plate. Tell the girls that the toothpaste tube represents the group and where we meet. The toothpaste is like the stories and personal information that is shared in the group (tube). Once you have all of the toothpaste squeezed onto the plate, ask the girls to use their wooden sticks to put all the toothpaste back into the tube. Encourage them to stay with the task and put all that information back into the tube of confidentiality. As the girls come to the conclusion that it can't be done agree with them that it can't and just like it is impossible to put the toothpaste back in the tube once it's out, it is also impossible to take words back once they have been spoken. Good friendships are built on trust and confidence so that when we share our secrets, our hopes and sometimes silly ideas the person we are sharing with will keep that information confidential, or just between us. Information in group needs to stay in the group because once it's shared outside the room our confidence in each other is broken and it can't be put back together.

CLOSING:

Go around the group and ask the girls to share one thing they learned in group today and one thing they hope to learn in the coming weeks. Close by telling the girls that in the next 7 weeks they will be exploring relationship styles in the girl's world and learn ways to be a good friend and to surround themselves with good friends by learning how to recognize positive relationship styles in themselves and others.

SESSION 2
Bee-Haviors

Getting Started:

A healthy bee hive is always abuzz with activity.

Every bee in the hive has a role and their place in the bee world. Bees rely on each other and almost always operate in a group; just like girls. Rosalind Wiseman defines these roles in the friendship hierarchy in her book, *Queen Bees and Wannabes.* None of the roles are inherently negative and there are strengths to the personalities of each individual role identified. Problems arise within the

This session invites girls to explore the strengths and pitfalls of each individual in their friendship hive.

roles when girls find themselves in unhealthy friendships and engage in maladaptive relationship styles. This session introduces the girls to the dominant roles in the girl's world and invites them to explore the strengths and pitfalls of each individual in their friendship hive.

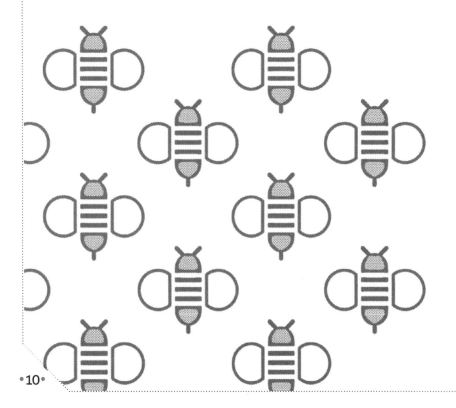

ACTIVITY 2.1
Introducing the Queen's Court

PURPOSE: Introduce the hierarchy roles in the hive and identify strengths and potential difficulties for each role.

OBJECTIVES: Group members will:

1. Understand the role of the Queen in the relational aggression hierarchy.

2. Identify unhealthy Queen bee behaviors and offer replacement behaviors.

RESOURCES/MATERIALS:
The Queen's Court Activity Sheet • Pen/pencil

PROCEDURES:

1. Introduce group members to the hierarchy of the bee hive and discuss how it relates to the unhealthy relationships girls can become involved in.

2. Ask the girls to follow along as you read each role.

3. Read each role and ask the girls to think about any similarities in their own friendship groups.

4. Discussion questions are included for deeper understanding.

Queen's Court
ACTIVITY SHEET

If you think you might be a Queen Bee, what are some ways you can "take off the crown"? List ways you could become a more positive leader.

_____

_____

_____

_____

_____

_____

If you know a Queen Bee, what would you recommend she do differently to be more positive?

_____

_____

_____

_____

_____

_____

_____

Queen Bee: Large and in Charge!

The honey bee Queen is about twice the length of the worker bees and she is definitely the 'boss of the hive'! She is the only honey bee that has the ability to sting multiple times without dying from the effect. She rarely leaves the comfort of the hive and depends on the bees around her to carry out her orders. She reigns supreme for an average of 2 years before she dies and another Queen takes her place.

Her human counter-part is also the 'boss of the hive'! She has an air around her that makes her seem larger than life. She can be affectionate and charming with certain people . . . when she needs to be; but she is also cruel and intolerant. She can argue anyone down, including friends, teachers, and parents. She gains power over those around her and uses them to carry out her orders. A Queen bee in the girl world will remain in "power" for approximately 2 years before her hostile and cruel behavior begins to wear on those around her and she loses her power over them (Faris and Felmlee, 2000).

Ask girls to make a list of strengths and pitfalls for the Queen bee.

Leader Note: Discuss the strengths and pitfalls the girls listed and share some of the following to guide the conversation:

Possible strengths:

- She is a leader.
- She can make friends and bring people together.

_____

_____

Possible pitfalls:

- She can lose her sense of self by working so hard to maintain her image.
- She can be extremely insecure about others, feeling they don't really like her but are using her popularity.
- She is very image conscious and depends on her relationships to give the impression that she has everything under control.

_____

_____

The Queen in Waiting

Every hive has a Queen in Waiting (QW) to take the place of the reigning Queen if she suddenly dies or is unable to complete her duties as Queen. The QW has all of the exact qualities of the Queen Bee and are treated with great respect-while allowed to live. If there is no need for the QW she is put to death by the hive as soon as she is fully developed because there can never be more than one Queen in any hive.

The QW in the human hive is second to the Queen, but can also be a target of the Queen. She always supports the Queen because she is her connection to power and will willingly lie for her to maintain power. She is often a mirror image of the Queen and allows her to tell her how to think, dress, and what to do; she allows herself to be pushed around by the Queen. Together the Queen and QW present the impression of impenetrable force and a solid friendship but this is no true friendship.

> **The Wannabee will do anything to be part of the Queen's Court and be connected with the Queen and the Queen in Waiting.**

This is a relationship of power and punishment that the Queen will strike down the QW at the slightest hint of disloyalty.

The Wannabee

The Wannabee will do anything to be part of the Queen's Court and be connected with the Queen and the QW. She knows that she does not hold the power of the QW but she is always on the lookout for a crack in the alliance of the Queen and QW so she can take the QW's place in the hive. She is a gossiper and a pleaser and will go to great lengths to increase her position and power within the Queen's Court-even purposely sabotage the friendship between the Queen and the QW. She doesn't have a personal opinion outside of what the Queen thinks. She is indecisive and reluctant to go against the Queen and the QW. She likes the feeling of belonging and not being a target, however she is gossiped about and used by the Queen and the QW. She is often chosen to carry out the dirty deeds of the Queen and will gladly take any punishment for the Queen's actions. She may appear to be the meanest and most vindictive girl in the Queen's court, but rarely is she acting on her own thoughts or desires.

Ask girls to make a list of strengths and pitfalls for the QW and Wannabee.

Leader Note: Discuss the strengths and pitfalls the girls listed and share some of the following to guide the conversation:

Possible strengths:

● She is loyal.

● She is dependable.

● She likes to make those around her happy and doesn't have to be the center of attention.

_____

_____

Possible pitfalls:

● She can be so focused on others opinions that she doesn't have a voice of her own.

● She can be pressured into doing things she wouldn't normally do just to fit in with the group.

● She can find it difficult to tell the difference between what she wants and what the group wants.

_____

_____

Questions for activity sheet:

List ways you could become a more positive leader.

_____

_____

_____

What could you say to a "Wannabee" to make her aware of her behavior?"

_____

_____

_____

CLOSING:

Thank girls for participating. Remind them about confidentiality and the importance for them to keep what is discussed in group in the room. Ask them to think about the three roles discussed in the session during the week and see if they observe any of the Queen Court behaviors in their friendships.

SESSION 3
The Working Class - Supporting Roles and Afraid to Bees

Getting Started:

In the world of the honey bee, the Queen is surrounded by workers that have many different roles in the hive. Worker bees are all female and they have many different jobs. The lifespan of a worker bee is about 6 weeks and her job will change as she gets older. The worker bee's only responsibility is to serve the Queen and the hive until she is no longer needed and her life is over.

Girls stuck in an unhealthy human hive can feel the same desperation as the worker bees in a honeybee hive. Girls can feel that even if they don't really like the hive or her role in the hive that she has no other options and without the hive she is nothing. For girls, having a best friend or a group of friends, and belonging to a group, is very important. Girls develop and build friendships by doing things together; the activities can either strengthen their relationships or harm them. Let's look at the different worker bee roles and see if we can find any comparisons to roles in the human hive.

For girls, having a best friend or a group of friends, and belonging to a group, is very important.

ACTIVITY 3.1
The Working Class - Supporting Roles and Afraid to Bees

PURPOSE: Introduce the hierarchy roles in the hive and identify strengths and potential difficulties for each role.

OBJECTIVES: Group members will:

1. Understand the supporting roles in the relational aggression hierarchy.

2. Identify unhealthy supporting role behaviors and offer replacement behaviors.

RESOURCES/MATERIALS:

The Working Class, Supporting Roles and Afraid to Bees Activity Sheet

PROCEDURES:

1. Introduce group to the hierarchy of the bee hive and discuss how it relates to the unhealthy relationships girls can become involved in.

2. Distribute the Working Class, Supporting Roles and Afraid to Bees Activity Sheet and ask the girls to follow along as you read each role.

3. Read the each role and ask the girls to think about any similarities in their own groups of friends.

4. Discussion questions are included for deeper understanding.

The Working Class

Forager Bees

Forager Bees are the oldest working bees in the hive and the only ones allowed to fly away from the hive. Their job is to gather nectar and pollen and bring it back to the group. The Forager Bee is similar to the Gossip and the Floater in the human hive. The Gossip gathers information on people like a Forager Bee gathers pollen. The Gossip takes the information back to the group and uses it to maintain her importance and popularity. She freely moves around from girl to girl and seems harmless on the surface, but everyone is afraid of her. The gossip tends to get girls to trust her and when she gets information, it doesn't seem like gossip. She becomes a listener, pretending to be a true friend, while using the information she gathers to further her own benefit. She has information on everyone that has mistakenly confided in her (this even includes the Queen Bee). She uses the information to cause conflict between people in order to secure her position in the hive. Once girls figure out what she's doing, they don't trust her and she can lose her power position in the group.

The Floater

The Floater is the exact opposite of the Gossip. The Floater is not connected to a single group of friends and moves freely between groups. People genuinely like and respect her, without feeling intimidated and they trust her with information. People confide in her and do not fear that she will use the information against them. The floater doesn't gain anything by creating conflict and insecurity in other girls like the Gossip does. She does not try to use information about others to increase her power and control with any group.

Discussion starter: Take a minute to think about gossip.

● What is gossip? Is gossip true or false? (Gossip is the act of spreading personal information, true or untrue, about someone to others.)

● Have you heard information about others that was untrue but believed it to be true?

● Have you told personal information about someone that they asked you to keep private or secret?

● Is it ok to tell something about someone else that you heard from another person even if you don't know if it is true?

● What are some ways you have seen gossip spread? (Face to face, Twitter, Instagram, Facebook, Vine)

● What are some things you could do to stop gossip or not participate in gossip?

● What can you do if you find out someone is gossiping about you?

"The Afraid to Bees"

The House Bee
The House Bee is the youngest, smallest and most vulnerable bee in the hive. The House Bee only serves in it's role for two days before being removed from the hive or moved on to a different worker role. For these two days the House Bee cleans around all the other worker bees in the hive. The only purpose for the House bee is to clean. This life of servitude can be compared to the roles of Torn Bystander and Target in the human hive. In unhealthy friendships, the Torn-Bystander and Target can experience great suffering due to the treatment they receive from the group.

The Torn Bystander
The Torn Bystander finds herself in a constant state of conflict with doing the right thing and being part of the group. She often apologizes or cleans up for the Queen's and others in the hive's behavior because she knows it's wrong but she feels caught in the middle. She may avoid activities because she's afraid others in the hive will make fun of her or try to pressure her to do things that make her uncomfortable. She is often in the background and won't commit to a side when there is conflict. She wants everyone to get along and tries to clean up everyone else's problems to keep the focus off of herself.

The Target

Like the House Bee, the Target is the most vulnerable individual in the group. She is often isolated and excluded from activities. She often feels pressured and humiliated by the group and helpless to stop other girls' behavior. She doesn't know how to stand up for herself and may be tempted to try to change herself to fit in with the group.

Refer the girls to their activity sheet and ask them to think about their friend groups as they answer the questions.

- Have you ever felt like you were just being used by your friends to clean up after them?

- Can you think of a time when you saw someone treat another girl badly, like a target? Did you step in or stay silent?

- Is it okay to join in and laugh at someone even if you know it is hurting their feelings?

- Have you ever stood up for someone even though you felt like what they were doing was wrong? How did that make you feel? What could you do instead?

- Why do you think girls act mean to other girls? What are some things you could do to stand up for someone?

- Have you ever felt like the target? How did you handle being the target? What are some things you could do if you were treated like a target in the future?

- Now that you have learned about all the roles in the hive, could you see yourself in any of them? Can you see your friends in any of those roles?

CLOSING:

Thank girls for participating. Remind them about confidentiality and the importance for them to keep what is discussed in group in the room. Ask them to think about the roles discussed during the week and see if they observe any of the supporting role behaviors in their friendships.

The Working Class, Supporting Roles and Afraid to Bees
ACTIVITY SHEET

🔶 Have you ever felt like you were just being used by your friends to clean up after them?

_____

_____

🔶 Can you think of a time when you saw someone treat another girl badly, like a target? Did you step in or stay silent?

_____

_____

🔶 Is it okay to join in and laugh at someone even if you know it is hurting their feelings?

_____

_____

🔶 Have you ever stood up for someone even though you felt like what they were doing was wrong? How did that make you feel? What could you do instead?

_____

_____

🔶 Why do you think girls act mean to other girls? What are some things you could do to stand up for someone?

_____

_____

🔶 Have you ever felt like the target? How did you handle being the target? What are some things you could do if you were treated like a target in the future?

_____

_____

🔶 Now that you have learned about all the roles in the hive, could you see yourself in any of them? Can you see your friends in any of those roles?

_____

_____

SESSION 4
The Bee in Me

Getting Started:

Discovering you are a part of a hive dynamic can be extremely difficult. It is important for girls to reflect on their personal tendencies and identify their primary role in the dynamic to confront the Hive culture in their relationships and move forward. Bees and young ladies are beautiful, hardworking and oftentimes misunderstood! The better they understand themselves, the more able they will be to avoid the traps of Life in the Hive and develop strong, healthy relationships.

The better girls understand themselves, the more able they will be to avoid the traps of Life in the Hive and develop strong, healthy relationships

ACTIVITY 4.1
The Bee in Me

PURPOSE: Allow girls to further explore their role in the relationship hierarchy.

OBJECTIVES: Group members will:

1. Identify their primary role and relational style tendencies.

2. Begin to self-reflect on their relationship style and identify healthy relationship patterns.

RESOURCES/MATERIALS:

The Bee in Me Quiz Activity Sheet

PROCEDURES:

1. Distribute the Bee in Me Quiz Activity Sheet and instruct girls to complete.

2. Allow girls time to complete quiz.

3. After the girls complete the quiz and review their results ask them to answer the four questions.

4. Invite girls to share their results and their thoughts about whether they feel they are accurate.

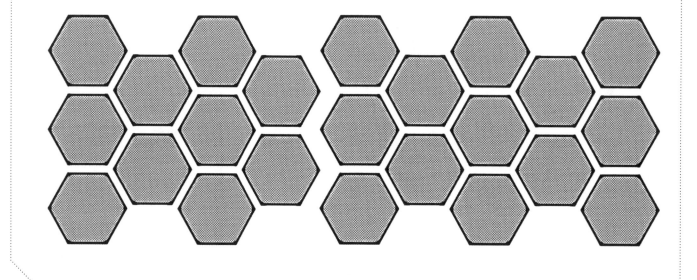

The Bee in Me Quiz

The following questions are designed to help you assess your role in the hive. For each question, select the one behavior that sounds most like you.

Attitudes

A. I believe connections to girls at home, school, and play are an important part of my life.

B. Other girls are often an "ends to a means," enabling me indirectly to get things I want for myself.

C. I am somewhat insecure and afraid of girls in my school.

D. I would choose to hang out with guys rather than girls, no matter what the activity.

Friendships

A. I have a lot of female friends.

B. I am often unhappy with the female friends I have.

C. I feel my female friends take advantage of me or abuse me.

D. There is an absence of female friends in my life.

Relationships

A. I respect and cooperate with girls, even if they're not individuals I consider as friends.

B. I am only interested in girls for what they can do for me or enable me to acquire for myself.

C. There are girls I know with whom I have positive relationships outside of my friends and family.

D. I only choose to interact with girls I know I can lead.

Behavior

A. I use many types of behaviors to interact with girls in my school throughout the day; most often relying on direct communication to interact with others.

B. I am often the girl who is "in the know," passing along what others tell me, staying on top of school happenings and using information to control others.

C. I usually allow others to call the shots, rarely speaking up for myself or expressing my true feelings.

D. I rarely worry about what others think.

Results

If the A statements describe you best...

You sound like a girl who has avoided the "Hive" style of interacting — congratulations!

If the B statements describe you best...

You may be trapped in a "Queens Court" role, participating passively in aggression or doing nothing to stop it.

If the C statements describe you best...

You may be trapped in an "Afraid-to-Bee" role, being bullied by other girls and lacking the strength to stand up against the "Hive."

If the D statements describe you best...

You may be trapped in a "Queen Bee" role, unaware that your interactions with other girls can be overly aggressive.

Overall, I can best identify with:

_____

_____

What are the feelings that control my relationships with other girls?

_____

_____

What are some behaviors that are common in my relationships with other girls?

_____

_____

What are three things that I can do to change these emotions or behaviors?

_____

_____

Adapted from: Dellasega, C. (2005). *Mean Girls Grown Up. Adult Women Who are Still Queen Bees, Middle Bees, and Afraid-to-Bees.* Hoboken, NJ: John Wiley & Sons, Inc.

SESSION 5
Bee-ing Me

Getting Started:

Defining healthy friendships can be challenging for young girls. Many girls lack the emotional tools to identify healthy friendships. Too often, their idea of friendship comes from the media and other outside influences that reinforce negative traits of adolescent friendships. A true friend holds up a mirror and allows us to see ourselves.

They are the ones who show us our strengths when all we see is weakness; they point out our positive characteristics, like courage and loyalty, when we are down on ourselves. They remind us of past accomplishments and encourage us. In healthy friendships, both individuals come away with a stronger sense of "self." Identifying the qualities of a healthy friendship through self-reflection empowers girls to seek out friendships that build them up rather than tear them apart.

Major elements of healthy teenage relationships are: respect, trust, mutual intimacy, caring and empathy, communication, and self-awareness/self-worth.

In order to have a good friend you have to bee a good friend. Through friendships, teens are able to empathize with others, experience both feelings of independence and dependence within a relationship, trust others, and communicate more easily in times of conflict. Major elements of healthy teenage relationships are: respect, trust, mutual intimacy, caring and empathy, communication, and self-awareness/self-worth.

ACTIVITY 5.1
Bee Me

PURPOSE: Girls will understand the meaning of a healthy friendship and how they are developed.

OBJECTIVES: Group members will:

1. Define aspects of healthy relationships.

2. Learn skills that promote healthy relationships.

RESOURCES/MATERIALS:

Friendship Flowers Activity Sheet • Pen/ Pencil • Colors (optional)

PROCEDURE:

1. Explain: A honeybee travels 3 miles a day and visits 50-100 flowers to gather the necessary ingredients to make honey. Beecoming a good friend requires combining many qualities of healthy friendships.

2. Instruct the girls to fill in the middle of each of the 5 flowers with a quality that they think makes a good friend. (For example, honesty, trust, encouragement, humor, forgiveness, loyalty, supportive, helpful)

3. When they have their middles filled in ask them to share the qualities they filled in with the group. During this time they can change or add to their responses.

4. After they have shared the qualities of a friend have them think about the acts that display each quality. In each of the flower petals have them write actions that would support or develop each quality. Encourage group members to list specific examples of behaviors not general concepts. (For example: Honesty: doesn't tell lies (even small white ones), tells you what they think and doesn't tell someone else something different, if they are hanging out with someone else they tell you the truth instead of making up a story. Supportive: understanding, a good listener, respectful, apologizes, doesn't embarrass or criticize, doesn't tease or pick on you. Helpful: helps you learn things, helps with school projects, gives good advice.

5. Ask the girls to share some of the specific behaviors they listed for each quality.

6. Distribute the colors and instruct the girls to pick out three colors they would like to use on their flowers (optional). Have them choose one color to represent each of the following responses: Easy for me, Somewhat difficult for me, and Very difficult for me.

7. Ask the girls to think about their friend groups specifically and consider the following questions:

● Which of the behaviors on the petals are easy for you, difficult for you and very difficult for you?

_____

_____

● When you think of your friends, are there some of these behaviors that you listed that they do really well in your friendship? Are there some that they aren't so good at?

_____

_____

● Which of the qualities do you think you do the best? Which areas would you like to improve?

_____

_____

● Now highlight the petals that you are committed to trying out with your friends to become the friend you want to bee.

_____

_____

CLOSING:

Encourage girls to try to live the behaviors and qualities they have come up with for healthy friendships. Stress to the group that practicing these behaviors will improve their friendships.

Friendship Flowers
ACTIVITY SHEET

In the middle of each flower write a quality of a good friendship.
On the petals surrounding each quality write actions that would show that quality.

SESSION 6
Bee-Long

Getting Started:

Bees in a hive are in a constant state of transformation that compares to the constant transformation in tweens and teens. Bees experience many developmental changes in a short timespan just as girls are experiencing major developmental changes in the teenage years. Girls are not only trying to figure out who they are, but also where they belong in their social structures. This can be a frightening time of identity crisis for young ladies. "Who am I? Where do I belong, My body feels different, I look different, people are reacting to me differently, none of the things I do work out the way they used to, and I don't know whether anyone likes me anymore." This is just a sample of the thoughts that go through the minds of young ladies embroiled in these transitions. Add to this inner turmoil the strong need to belong to a group and things can be emotionally messy!

> **Girls are not only trying to figure out who they are, but also where they belong in their social structures.**

ACTIVITY 6.1
My Hive

PURPOSE: Girls will explore their self-identity and their belonging in social groups.

OBJECTIVES: Group members will:

1. Consider the many aspects and uniqueness of their identity.

2. Learn different ways that people define personal identity and things they have in common.

3. Develop self-esteem by identifying personal support structures.

RESOURCES/MATERIALS:

My Hive Activity Sheet • Markers/Colors/Colored Pencils

PROCEDURES:

1. Distribute the My Hive activity sheet and ask the girls to fill out each area of the Honey Comb with words that describe who they are in each area.

2. Explain that personal identity and a sense of belonging is developed as you grow up relating to particular people in particular places with particular experiences. For example, you identify as part of your family (daughter, sister, granddaughter, cousin, aunt). You identify as a part of a community because you are a citizen. In school you identify as a student. If you join a team or club you take on "team member" as part of your identity.

3. Have the girls share their hives with the group and have them compare their similarities and differences. Ask the girls if there are any areas of their hive they would like to expand or grow. Discuss ways that they can accomplish their goals to expand areas of their hive.

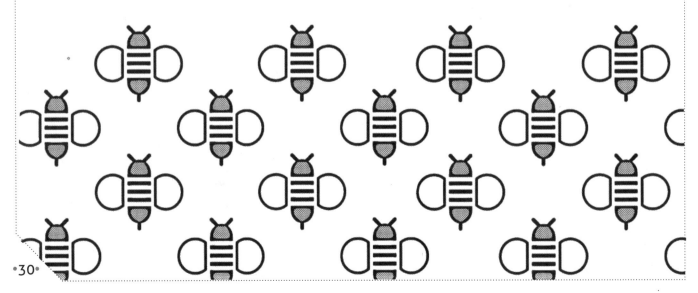

My Hive
ACTIVITY SHEET

Fill in each area of the hive with words that describe your membership or identity in each area.

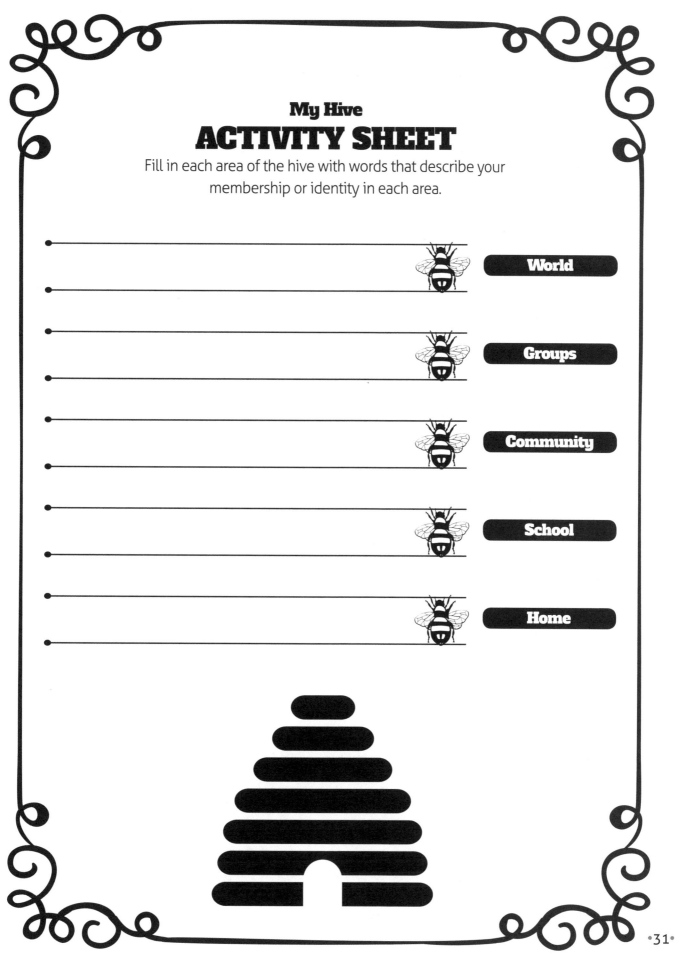

World

Groups

Community

School

Home

ACTIVITY 6.2
We Bee-Long

PURPOSE: Girls will explore their self-identity and their belonging in social groups.

OBJECTIVES: Group members will:

1. Discuss the importance of belonging to a group of friends.

2. Discuss ways to maintain personal identity within friend groups.

RESOURCES/MATERIALS:

We Bee-Long Activity Sheet • Pen/ Pencil

PROCEDURE:

1. Instruct the girls to get in pairs and list as many items as they can that bee-long together on their Bee-long activity sheet. Give examples like peanut butter and jelly, Oreos and milk, pizza and soda, popcorn and butter, bees and honey, etc.

2. When they have finished ask them to look at their list and discuss whether some of the things listed don't go together for them. For example, some people don't like butter on their popcorn.

3. Have the girls look at their hives and consider the groups they belong to. Have they experienced benefits and problems with any of their specific groups?

4. Ask the girls to think about their friend groups specifically and consider the following questions:

● Are there some times that you and your friends don't bee-long together? (For example, you might not all play the same sport, live in the same neighborhood, or like the same foods).

● Have you ever felt pressured to do something with a group of friends that you did not want to do?

● Why do you think girls sometimes do things that they do not want to do when they are around their friends?

● Why do you think it is difficult for people to say "No" to their friends?

● Do you think there are times when it is better not to change, just to bee-long?

● What are some reasons that would cause you to choose not to bee-long to a group?

● Have the girls return to their Hive activity sheet and add the reasons they wrote down to not bee-long.

● Explain that by identifying reasons they would not bee-long to a group they are defining their personal boundaries. As they continue to develop their personal identity it is important to try to maintain those boundaries so they do not find themselves stuck in a group they don't really feel comfortable bee-longing to.

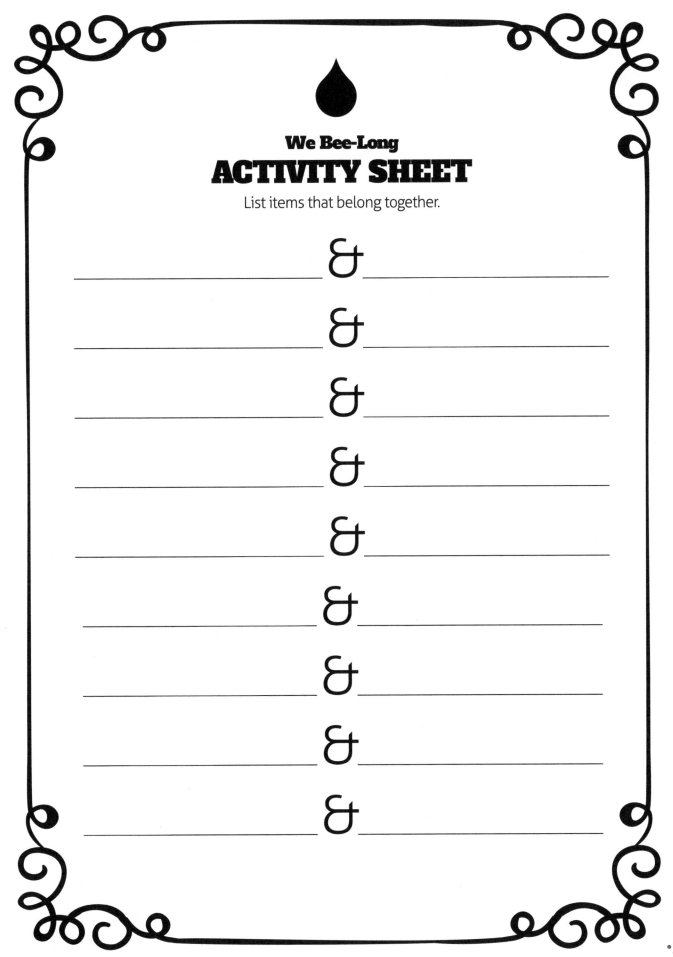

We Bee-Long
ACTIVITY SHEET
List items that belong together.

_____ & _____

_____ & _____

_____ & _____

_____ & _____

_____ & _____

_____ & _____

_____ & _____

_____ & _____

_____ & _____

SESSION 7
Bee-Lieve

Getting Started:

Sticks and Stones may break your bones but names can never hurt you. We have all heard this old adage, but growing up girls, we know it to be fundamentally false. Now there is brain research to support that emotional pain-like the pain words cause-is processed in the same area of the brain in girls and women that processes physical pain. So, in essence, words sting us in the same way a broken bone does. In the bee world only female bees have the ability to sting. There is great cost to the worker bee if they use their stinger; because they have a barbed stinger, the stinger gets lodged in the skin of its victim. This is fatal to the bee when they try to pull away from the victim, and the bee will die after the stinging incident. Similarly, we can lose a bit of ourselves when we use stinging words that harm our friendships.

In essence, words sting us in the same way a broken bone does.

ACTIVITY 7.1
Stingers and Zingers

PURPOSE: Group members will begin thinking about the power behind the words we use and the lasting effect words can have on us as individuals.

OBJECTIVES: Group members will:

1. Discuss the power in the words they use.

2. Evaluate the words they use with their friends and in relationships.

RESOURCES/MATERIALS:

Sheet of clean, unblemished computer paper for each group member.

PROCEDURES:

1. As girls enter the room hand them a piece of paper and tell them to take very good care of it. As if it was their very best friend.

2. Play the following video before beginning the activity: Words Hurt: http://www.youtube.com/watch?v=1j6YA03hm4k&list=PLDD3DB7E70C9CC3AC

3. Tell girls that they will be talking about the importance of words and what we believe about ourselves and others. Ask them to take their piece of paper and crumple it up, stomp on it, really mess it up but do not rip it.

4. Have them unfold the paper, smooth it out and look at it. How is it different than when you first gave it to them? Is it scarred and dirty? What can they do to fix it?

5. Ask the girls to tell the piece of paper they're sorry. Did their apology fix the paper and return it to its original state?

6. Tell the girls that even though you said you were sorry, and tried to fix the paper, look at all the scars left behind. Those scars will never go away no matter how hard you try to fix it. This is what happens when we use our words out of anger or to gain popularity or revenge by putting down others. You may say you are sorry, but the scars on the individual that the words were targeted toward can last forever.

Ask: Do you have scars left behind by words that people have said to you? Take a minute to write down some of those words that have left you scarred on the sheet of paper.

Next, cross out the hurtful words and replace them with an opposite, positive word. Let the positive word take the place of the hurtful word. The more we counter the hurtful words with our own power words the better able we are to think positively about ourselves and begin to heal from the words that have sliced our souls.

What we believe about ourselves influences our interactions with each other. Many times we use words to hurt those closest to us because we are hurting. In order for us to have healthy friendships we have to be healthy ourselves. We can start healing the wounds of words by focusing on the good things about ourselves. When we recognize what is good about each of us we are better able to recognize the good in others.

ACTIVITY 7.2
Buzz Words: Sugar and Spice

PURPOSE: Group members will learn positive self-thought with positive words group members use to describe them.

OBJECTIVES: Group members will:

1. Use encouraging words with each other.

2. Have a list of positive words that describe them.

RESOURCES/MATERIALS:

Sticky notes for each girl. They will need two for each member in the group. (Each girl in a group of 8 would need 14 sticky notes (they won't write one for themselves)

Music

PROCEDURES:

1. Ask girls if anyone has ever talked about them behind their backs. Ask them if the talk behind their backs is always bad. Do they only say bad things about other people when they are not around? Do they ever say anything positive about their friends when they aren't around? Some of their responses should include that they "take up" for their friends around other people; that they do say positive things about others when they aren't around. Ask if they think their friends say nice things about them behind their backs. What do they think their friends say more, positive or negative things behind their back. Again, remind them that what we think influences how we respond to others. While it is true that we can't control everything that everyone says behind our backs, we can control our own thoughts and reactions. With that in mind ask the girls to think of two positive words to describe the other girls in the group.

2. Write one positive word on each sticky note to describe the girls in the group. Remember, you will actually be writing two words for each girl, but they need to be written on separate sticky notes.

3. After a few minutes have the girls stand up and stick their sticky notes on their fingers. Tell them they will be "talking behind each other's backs." Instruct them that when the music starts they will walk around the room and stick their words on each girl's back.

4. When all the girls have finished putting their words on each other's backs ask them to take their seats.

5. Once all girls are seated ask them to take out the scarred piece of paper and stick the words from their backs on to the paper.

6. Have the girls read the words to the group and share how the words make them feel. Were they surprised by any of the words? Can/do they believe the words?

7. Ask the girls to put the words in a folder or binder and commit to keeping it with them for the next week. Challenge them to read the words to themselves at least once a day until the next session.

CLOSING:

Remind the girls that what they believe about themselves really can influence how they treat others. Positive thoughts about themselves will help them focus on the positive in others. Encourage them to read the buzz words that the group wrote about them and allow those words to navigate their thoughts. As those words encourage them they will be better prepared to encourage others and that is one of the characteristics of a good friend!

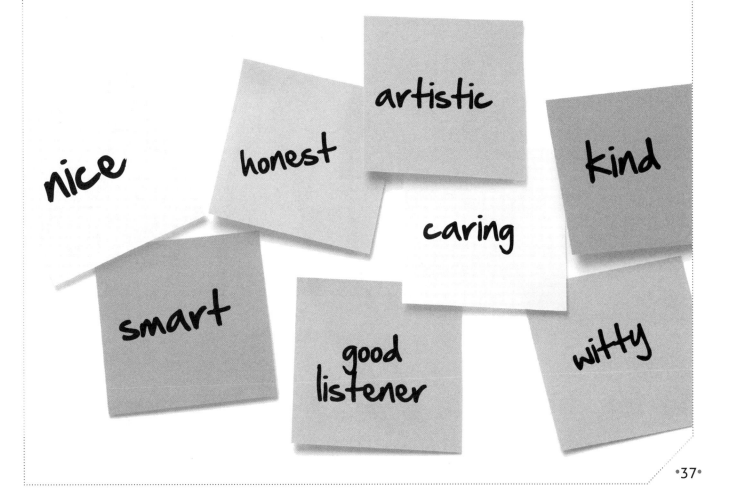

SESSION 8
Bee-Coming a Good Friend

Getting Started:

Welcome girls back and ask them if they read their buzz words during the week. Ask the girls that did read the words each day if they noticed any difference in their mood or thoughts during the week. Encourage girls that did not read their buzz words to keep them close and refer to them when they are feeling frustrated or discouraged. Our final session encourages girls to think about what they have learned in the group and how they will apply concepts in building healthy friendships.

Have girls apply concepts in building healthy friendships from what they have learned.

ACTIVITY 8.1
Creating a Healthy Hive

PURPOSE: Bring closure to the group.

OBJECTIVES: Group members will:

1. Reflect on what they learned about healthy friendships.

2. Set goals for applying what they have learned to their relationships.

3. Bring closure to the group.

RESOURCES/MATERIALS:

Paper • Pen/ Pencil

PROCEDURE:

1. Hand out a sheet of paper to each girl and ask her to fold it into three parts. Tear along each crease to make three separate pieces of paper.

2. Instruct girls to write the following topics on each piece of paper:

- One thing I learned in group that I didn't know before.
- One thing I learned about myself in group.
- One thing I will try to do to be a better friend.

3. Give the girls a chance to write a response to each of the questions and then instruct them to wad up their responses.

4. Have the girls throw their wadded up responses into the middle of the group.

5. Ask each group member to pick up three of the papers from the pile.

6. Ask the girls to read the responses aloud and discuss.

CLOSING:

Reinforce the girls' participation in group and encourage them to apply what they learned. Encourage them to talk with each other outside of group and to feel comfortable reaching out to you.

THRIVE

IN THE HIVE

APPENDIX WITH
OPTIONAL ACTIVITIES

ACTIVITY 9.1
Perception Deception

OVERVIEW: This activity encourages girls to think about how their perceptions impact their relationships.

PURPOSE: Understand how perception shapes behavior.

OBJECTIVES: As a result of this activity, group members will:
1. Learn how perception can hurt relationships.

RESOURCES/MATERIALS:
Paper • Pen/ Pencil •Small rubber balls for each pair of girls

PROCEDURE:

1. Have girls break into pairs.

2. Tell group that they are going to complete three tasks with their partners.

First, have one partner take the ball and toss it in the air and catch it. They can also toss it back and forth with other pairs. Instruct the partner that does not have the ball to write down everything that she sees her partner doing. After 60 seconds have the girls change roles and have the writing partner toss the ball and the partner with the ball do the writing for another 60 seconds.

Next, instruct one of the girls to tell their schedule to their partner and instruct the partner to write down what they say. After 60 seconds have them reverse roles for 60 seconds.

Finally, instruct one of the girls to think about their favorite things and have their partner write down what they are thinking. After 60 seconds have them reverse roles for 60 seconds.

3. After they have completed all 3 activities have the girls come back to the group and ask the following questions:

- Which activity was the easiest to complete? Why? (Typical responses will be recording what the partner was doing and what they were saying.)

- Which activity was the most difficult to complete? Why? (Typical response will be trying to record what the partner was thinking.)

- Have you ever found yourself making an assumption about what someone else was thinking based on what they were doing or saying? If yes, do you think your perception of what they were thinking was correct? Why?

- Has anyone every made an assumption that they knew what you were thinking? Were they correct?

- How can your perception that you know what someone is thinking harm a friendship?

ACTIVITY 9.2
Honey Chain

PURPOSE: Recognize how similarities and differences between group members can strengthen their relationships.

OBJECTIVES: Group members will:
1. Recognize that similarities and differences contribute to healthy friendships.
2. Value individual uniqueness in a friend.

RESOURCES/MATERIALS:

Yellow strips of construction paper (approximately 1.25 to 1.5 inches wide) • Glue Sticks
Pen/ Pencil

PROCEDURE:
1. Provide paper strips to each girl. (Number of strips will be determined by number of girls in the group. Each group member will need one strip to represent each of the group members).
2. Ask girls to think of ways they are similar to and different from the other girls in the group.
3. Instruct girls to talk with each other and write down one similarity and one difference they have with each other. (If girls are having difficulty, give some examples of ways that people may be different or similar, such as hair color/eye color, birth order, number of siblings, extra-curricular activities, age, favorite singer/band, favorite TV show, favorite food, etc.)
4. Allow girls time to identify and write similarities and differences for each member before moving on.
5. Ask girls to share two ways she is similar and two ways she is different from the other girls in the group.
6. After the first girl shares, start a chain by overlapping and gluing together the ends of one of her strips and have her add the rest of her strips to the chain.
7. As each girl shares pass the glue stick to her and ask her to continue the chain with her strips until all girls have added their strips to the chain.
8. As the chain grows encourage girls to reflect on the many things they have in common, as well as the ways that each person in the group is unique.
9. Ask the girls to think about their friends and their similarities and differences and consider the following questions:
   - How do similarities benefit friendships?
   - How do differences between people make friendships stronger?
   - What are ways to "connect" with others who may be a little bit different from you?
10. Tell girls that even though members of the group may be different, in many ways they are the same. Hang the Honey Chain in the room or around the doorway as a reminder of the similarities and uniqueness that each girl contributes to the group and their individual friendships.

ACTIVITY 9.3
Buzz, Buzz, Buzz

PURPOSE: Identify and explore different "cliques" in the school and how stereotypes can hurt relationships.

OBJECTIVES: Group members will:

1. Identify cliques that they define in their school or community.

2. Understand how stereotypes can be incorrect and harmful to building a positive culture.

RESOURCES/MATERIALS:

Flip chart paper or large pieces of butcher paper • Markers

PROCEDURE:

1. Explain that similar to the many roles or groups in a bee hive, there are many different groups in a school community. There are groups like athletes, band, drama club, ROTC, student council, etc. that are organized by the school. There are also informal groups that the student body defines like, preps, kickers, emo, stoners, nerds that are rarely positive.

2. Ask the girls to identify some of the informal groups in the school that they are aware of.

3. Label the top of each sheet of paper with the name of a different type of group the girls identify.

4. Instruct the girls to write on each sheet of paper one thing that they either "know" or have heard about the people or group. (Emphasize that they are not to write individual names on any of the papers, only traits or general beliefs of each group).

5. After all girls have had a chance to write on each sheet give them a few minutes to read what was written about each group.

Once they have had a chance to read each sheet, ask the following questions:

- Are the comments written on each sheet primarily positive or negative?
- Why do you think that is?
- Are the comments all true? How do you know?
- Would you want to be a part of these groups? How do these labels influence how you interact or feel about people that are perceived to be a part of each group?
- Do you want to be defined by stereotypes? What are some ways you could break out of a stereotype?

Talk with the girls about stereotypes and how we become conditioned to think about individuals based on the clique they are in and stereotypes almost automatically whether the stereotype is true or not. When we base our desire to get to know someone or be their friend based on what we hear or think about them because of a clique or stereotype we miss opportunities to have rich friendships with others. In order to avoid letting stereotypes define what we think about people; it is important that we begin to become conscious of the fact that we are often thinking about people based on the "buzz" we hear about them. We must stop believing the "buzz" and ask ourselves if what we are thinking is a fact or a stereotype.

It is important that we begin to become conscious of the fact that we are often thinking about people based on the "buzz" we hear about them.

ACTIVITY 9.4
Behind the Green Lantern (Jealousy)

Getting Started:

Jealousy is a normal human emotion and we all feel jealous from time to time. It is when jealous feelings are not addressed that they become destructive to friendships. Girls are more prone to jealousy in friendships because they have higher expectations for loyalty, commitment, and empathy from their friends. Girls can become jealous within their friendships for many reasons, but one of the most anxiety-causing experiences is sharing a friend. Most girls can handle the frustrations associated with sharing friends; but there are some who have enormous difficulties navigating this challenging situation. Girls

> **Girls are more prone to jealousy in friendships because they have higher expectations for loyalty, commitment, and empathy from their friends.**

who are stuck in unhealthy friendship groups often do not have the skills to handle the risks associated with sharing friends with others. They are the most prone to feeling threatened and vulnerable in their relationships with peers. When one person in a friendship experiences jealousy, it is a signal that something in the friendship needs to be communicated and addressed. Helping girls identify when they are feeling jealous can help them to communicate the cause of these feelings and address them in positive rather than destructive ways.

PURPOSE: Recognize how jealousy can harm friendships.

OBJECTIVES: Group members will:

1. Identify individual insecurities that cause jealousy in friendships.

2. Become more self-aware and counter identified insecurities with healthy communication.

RESOURCES/MATERIALS:

Behind the Green Lantern Activity Sheet

Brown paper bags (can use a variety of sizes depending on items in each)

Six Small items to place in each bag (i.e. small teddy bear, rubber ball, Q-tip, banana, play-doh, spoon, paperclip, rock, etc.)

Pen/ Pencil

PROCEDURE:

1. Number six paper bags with small items and place them on a table.

2. Hand out the Behind the Green Lantern Activity Sheet.

3. Ask girls to feel inside each paper bag without looking and write down three words to describe what they feel and write a possible answer of what is in the bag based on what they feel.

4. Allow girls time to identify and write descriptions for each item.

5. After the girls have had a chance to feel each item and write down their answers ask them to share some of the words they used to describe each item and then reveal what is in each bag.

6. Share with the group that sometimes we feel things that we can recognize without actually seeing them. Jealousy is an emotion that we oftentimes feel, but can struggle to identify. Jealousy is referred to as the "green-eyed monster" and when we look at our friends or our friendships through the green lantern of jealousy we can act out in toxic ways.

7. Ask the girls to think about a time they felt jealous and consider the following questions:

● What are some of the things that might cause you to be jealous in a friendship?

● How have you seen jealousy affect friendships?

● What have you seen people do when they are jealous?

● What is something you can do when you begin to feel jealous?

8. Encourage girls to identify jealousy for what it is when they begin to feel it. Say "Just like the items in the bags, we can feel jealousy rear its ugly head inside ourselves. If we name the feeling we can take control over it before it controls us and causes damage to our friendships." Offer girls some healthy strategies for taming their jealousy such as talking about it with a trusted adult, journaling, or sharing the feeling that is causing the jealousy with their friend. These are all healthy ways to deal with the normal feelings of jealousy that can occur in friendships.

Behind the Green Lantern
ACTIVITY SHEET

Feel each item in the paper bags and write down three words to describe what you feel. Write down your best guess of what item is in each bag.

Item 1: _____, _____, _____

Item 1 Answer _____

Item 2: _____, _____, _____

Item 2 Answer _____

Item 3: _____, _____, _____

Item 3 Answer _____

Item 4: _____, _____, _____

Item 4 Answer _____

Item 5: _____, _____, _____

Item 5 Answer _____

Item 6: _____, _____, _____

Item 6 Answer _____

The items in each bag were hidden from sight but easy to identify by feeling them. Jealousy is an emotion that can be hard to see, but we know it when we feel it. List three feelings you have when you are jealous _____, _____, _____

List three things you can you do when you begin to feel jealous? _____

_____

_____

_____

ACTIVITY 9.5
To Bee or Not to Bee – Role Play Scenarios

PURPOSE: Provide girls with the opportunity to discuss potential situations where relational aggressive behaviors could occur and practice using positive, healthy relational skills.

OBJECTIVES: Group members will:

1. Practice healthy communication in friendships.

2. Discuss personal responses to difficult situations and identify alternative behaviors.

RESOURCES/MATERIALS:

Role-play Scenarios

PROCEDURE:

1. Select a role-play scenario and share it with the group.

2. Ask for volunteers to act out the scenario and end the role play before choosing an ending. Discuss the different response options and then ask them to choose one (they may choose one of the endings included or create their own). Tell the girls that they can create their own dialogue for the ending.

3. Ask the audience to observe the actors respectfully and tell them they will have an opportunity to share their thoughts when the scene is complete.

4. Allow time for discussion following each scenario. With each discussion the facilitator can have the girls discuss the scenario from different perspectives to identify different responses for each individual in the role-play.

5. Optional: Ask the girls to write down situations they have seen between girls. You can use these situations to create additional role-play scenarios.

ROLE PLAY SCENARIOS

Difficult Decisions:

Jill and Sara have plans for Friday night to go to the movies and then stay at Jill's house. On Thursday, Sara's friend Olivia calls and tells her that her dad won tickets to a concert on Friday night and invites Sara to go with her. The concert is one that Sara would love to see. What should Sara do? Stop the role play and talk about the following possible responses.

Options:

1. Sara talks to Jill about her dilemma and asks if they can go to the movies another night and then goes to the concert with Olivia.

2. Sara thanks Olivia for the invitation but says that she already has plans for Friday night.

3. Sara accepts the invitation from Olivia to the concert and tells Jill she can't go to the movies and spend the night because she has to go to her grandma's house.

4. Choose your own ending.

Lunch Room Rules:

You and your group of friends are sitting at "your" lunch room table, the spot you have been sitting since freshman year. Two new girls come and sit at the table so there isn't room for all of your usual friends. Stop the role play and talk about the following possible responses.

Options:

1. Clearly the girls are confused as to the unwritten lunch room "rules" so you and your friends decide to educate them about where they can sit.

2. You and your friends make rude comments about the girls just loud enough so they can hear you so they will get the point that they are in the wrong place and move.

3. You make room and include the girls; it is only two spots after all.

4. Choose your own ending.

Time Share:

Brooke and Jennifer have been best friends since seventh grade. Now, starting freshman year they don't have any classes together and only see each other at lunch. Jennifer has three classes with Izzy and invited her to sit with her and Brooke at lunch. Jennifer and Izzy tried to include Brooke in their conversation, but Brooke was distant and didn't really talk. After lunch Brooke posted an embarrassing picture of Jennifer on her cell phone with the description, "Former BFF." Stop the role play and talk about the following possible responses.

Options:

1. Jennifer posts pictures of Brooke that would embarrass her.

2. Jennifer finds Brooke during the next passing period and lets her know what she thinks about the post and the comment in front of everyone.

3. Jennifer calls Brooke after school and invites her to go get a soda and talk about the picture and the comment.

4. Choose your own ending.

Stop the Drama:

During math class Emily tells Amanda that she heard Val talking about Amanda in the English class she has with her. Emily says, "I was so surprised by what Val was saying about you because I thought you were friends." Emily proceeds to give Amanda examples of what Val was saying. After class Amanda confronts Val about what Emily told her and Val tells her she didn't say any of those things about her and Emily was making it all up. Stop the role play and talk about the following possible responses.

Options:

1. Amanda tells Val she is a terrible friend and never wants to talk to her again.

2. Amanda believes her friend Val and the next time Emily starts to say things about Val she will tell Emily to stop and not listen to gossip.

3. Amanda and Val talk to Emily together and ask her not to make things up about them anymore.

4. Choose your own ending.

Crossing the Line:

Latoya tells her friend Sophie that she really likes Dillon and that they have been talking. During passing period Latoya sees Sophie walking in the hall and talking with Dillon. She thinks Sophie is walking a little too close and seems very interested in everything Dillon has to say. Stop the role play and talk about the following possible responses.

Options:

1. Latoya tweets about Sophie and all the boys she likes.

2. Latoya starts a rumor about Sophie and some guy she dated over the summer.

3. Latoya talks with Sophie and tells her it made her uncomfortable seeing her talking to Dillon.

4. Choose your own ending.

Thrive in the Hive Permission Form

Date: _____

From: _____

Dear Parent/Guardian,

Your daughter has been selected to participate in an eight week girls' group titled, Thrive in the Hive. Being part of a girls' group is an excellent way for girls to learn new skills, develop self-confidence, become more aware of how others see them, practice new behaviors, and better understand how to build healthy friendships.

This group will take place during the school day at a time that is least disruptive to the students' academic process. Please complete this consent form, either granting or denying permission for your child to participate in this group.

Please return the attached form to _____ (Insert Name) on or before

_____ (Insert date).

Thank you,

_____

Signature

_____ Grade _____

Student's Name

_____ I consent for my child to participate in the Thrive in the Hive girls' group.

_____ I Do Not consent for my child to participate in the Thrive in the Hive girls' group.

_____ _____

Parent Signature   Date

References

Besag, V. E. (2006). Bullying among girls friends or foes? *School Psychology International*, 27: 535-551.

Brown, L. M., & Gilligan, C. (1992). Meeting at the Crossroads: Women's Psychology and Girls' development. New York: Ballantine Books.

Crick, N. R., and Dodge, K. A. (1994). A review and reformulation of social information-processing mechanisms in children's social adjustment. *Psychol. Bull.* 115: 74–101.

Harris, J. R. (1995) 'Where is the child's environment? A group theory of socialisation', *Psychological Review* 97: 114–21.

Paddock, C. (2013, February 20). "Language Protein In Brain Differs By Sex." *Medical News Today*.

Savin-Williams, R. C. (1980) Social interactions of adolescent females in natural groups, in H. C. Foot, A. J. Chapman and J. R. Smith (eds.) Friendship and Social Relations in Children. Chichester: John Wiley

Simmons, R. (2002) Odd Girl Out: The Hidden Culture of Aggression in Girls. San Diego, CA: Harcourt Trade Publishing.

Underwood, M. K. (2003). Social Aggression Among Girls. New York: The Guilford Press.

Werner, N. E., and Nixon, C. L. (2005). Normative Beliefs and Relational Aggression: An investigation of the cognitive bases of adolescent aggressive behavior. *Journal of Youth and Adolescence*, Vol. 34, No. 3, pp. 229–243.

Wiseman, R. (2002) Queen Bees and Wannabes: Helping Your Daughter Survive Cliques, Gossip, Boyfriends and Other Realities of Adolescence. London: Judy Piakus (Publishers) Limited.

About the Author

Steph Jensen is currently the Director of Community Contracts for Boys Town in Boys Town, NE. She has eighteen years' experience as a classroom teacher, reading specialist, administrator, education consultant, trainer and national speaker. During the past eleven years, Ms. Jensen has conducted workshops for general and special educators across the country on best approaches to school-wide behavior management, strategies for the success of all students and relational aggression/bullying. She has conducted specialized training for staff working in juvenile justice and residential settings including applied evidence based behavior intervention strategies internationally with Japanese Child Welfare. She is knowledgeable about leadership change, school improvement and professional development. Her approaches are based on a solid knowledge of behavioral science, effective schools literature, and social learning theory.

Ms. Jensen is known for bringing an informed, passionate, and practical approach, as she works closely with school staff to decrease bullying and improve school climate, creating safe and productive school communities.